THOUGHTS ABOUT THINGS

Innovative Ideas About Business & Careers, from the Author of The Money Button

Brian Pittenger

Thoughts About Things

First Edition

ISBN 978-1-7320894-2-6

eISBN 978-1-7320894-3-3

2019-1

TABLE OF CONTENTS

THOUGHTS ABOUT IMPROVEMENT...87

THOUGHTS ABOUT HOW THINGS ARE CHANGING.....................................107

CHAPTER TWENTY-EIGHT: The Future of Business
Education

I need all of you to stop what you're doing and listen to me.

- *Ron Burgandy[i]*

PROLOGUE

When I finished the writing process for my first book, it was not called *The Money Button*. What is was called I won't reveal here, but needless to say it turns out it violated multiple copyright laws. Needless to say, I was trying hard to sell that book and thought that a title that would really 'pop' on Google's search engine would help it along.[1]

Anyway, it had a different title. And, it had a wildly different structure. It turns out that when you write a book, the next step in the process is to turn it over to your editors. Now, what's important to know here is that your editors will hate your book. That shouldn't be surprising, because everybody involved with your book will eventually come to hate your book. You, in fact, are the person who hates your book the most. That's something they don't tell you when you take your first English class in college, but it's true. You hate your book, and not just a little – a lot. Because, in the act of writing your book, you have to read that book, like, three thousand times. No book gets better with repetition, I assure you, and *your* book is no prize to start with. As you read and re-read the book, correcting errors, you will come across entire sections that appear to have been written by blinded vandal monkeys[2] who broke into your house while you were away and deliberately ran their butts over your keyboard for about six minutes. It's that bad.

---

[1] Okay, it was called *Dallas Cowboys McDonalds Ruby Rose, by Dan Brown*
[2] Which are real. And, would also make a great name for a band.

Now imagine being your editors. Except, they can't tell you how bad your writing is, at least not to your face. Instead they say things like, "Wow! This is a great start!" and "So few people actually get all the way through the writing process." Notice that neither of these things is, actually, a compliment.

So your editors make 'suggestions' almost immediately, and those suggestions are not subtle, though they are always formed as if they are questions, as there was clearly some sort of training in Editor school that said this is more polite. They ask things like, "Do you think the book should have more complete sentences?" and such. In my case, entire chapters moved from the back part of the book to the front, chapters were pulled out and others were added back in. The entire name of the book changed in the editing process where we 'found the book[3]' and the number of pages decreased from about 350 down to 200. Those changes have now made me a multi-millionaire famous book writer, of course, so it all worked out great.

But, in doing so, I lost some chapters that didn't fit into the theme of *The Money Button* but that are now going to make up the structure of *this* book. Here are some fun facts for you to consider as you read:

1) By definition, you are now reading a book whose entirety was built from sections that were not good enough for the first book.[4]

---

[3] This is another thing you hear during the editing process: "We found the book!" Because, it turns out, the thing you turned in to them in the first place, which *you* called your book, was actually *not* a book at all, but some horrible crime against grammar and syntax. Until, of course, your editors 'find' the book, at which point it becomes a book again, no thanks to you.

[4] For those of you who *read* the first book, I can't imagine that this is encouraging news. No refunds.

2) You'll notice all of these chapters are very short. I mean, *very* short. My last book was over 200 pages and just 10 chapters[5]. Turns out that my editors tell me business books don't need to be so long, and you can publish pretty much any length tomb if you can come up with some sort of fancy schmancy theme. Cool!

3) In spite of that, I did *not* actually come up with any such theme for this book[6]. Rather, this one is much more loosely tied together than the last book (which was, again, a masterwork of its time). Each chapter is basically just a brain dump of something I've thought about a lot and repeated to friends and employees over-and-over-and-over again over the years. They didn't seem to run away pulling out their ears to avoid hearing the sound of my voice, so why should you be any better? Huh? Is that what you're saying – you're better than my friends? 'Cause you're not, okay[7]?

So there you go! My new book. I do want this to be helpful, so of course consider what I've written here the start to a dialogue. I'd love to hear from you, so please find different ways to connect with me in the acknowledgements section.

Enjoy!

---

[5] You're welcome!

[6] Or, as my editors probably believe, we did *not* find the book.

[7] Look, yeah, some of you are bound to be better than my friends. That's ... that's just math, right?

THOUGHTS ABOUT
ATTITUDE

CHAPTER ONE:

Missed Opportunities

I've argued in the past that dysfunction is nothing unusual in large companies. It's particularly true in turnarounds. You will run into people who literally cannot see their way to a different solution for their problems, even when all the assets for successful change are right in their hands.

I call this the Peanut Butter Sandwich and Jelly Sandwich problem. Confused?

Let's see if I can help. Have you ever known anybody who faced this situation: They have a slice of bread in their right hand that has peanut butter all over it. And, they have a slice of bread in their left hand that has jelly spread across it. They look at you and say, "I just don't have *time* to eat two sandwiches!"

And, so, they simply do not eat.

Sigh.[8]

---

[8] This concept was inspired by a good friend of mine. By inspired, I mean she came up with it completely. However, I told her right away I was stealing it forever, thereby satisfying all laws and requirements per the case of *Dibs vs. Ferguson, 1976*. So, there – lawyered.

CHAPTER TWO:

We've All Got Reasons

I've given a lot of feedback in my life[9], received plenty, and coached those who've received their own feedback but didn't know what to do with it. When people are struggling and being called out for it, the most frequent reaction is for people to respond back to me with their 'reasons' why things aren't going their way.

Oh, our reasons! Here are some Greatest Hits:

- This particular partner was not helpful.
- Team Member X wasn't as productive as we hoped.
- You cut my budget.
- The company prioritized other things than my project.
- You and the other executives of this company deliberately attempted to murder me.[10]

The reasons go on-and-on.

So, here's the big blow: I don't give a shit. Not one. I either believe in you, or I don't. I either want to invest in you, or I'm done with you. Is my attitude cold? Yeah. Ruthless? Maybe.

I once had just joined a company and found that one of the Managers on my team, a 3-year employee of the organization,

---

[9] Boy, howdy, have I.
[10] Whiners.

had zero support. None. People were actively working against him.

I joined at the time of annual reviews and his had been co-written by my predecessor in the job and the VP of Finance. As I read this review to the Manager, I told him that I had rarely seen a review with such strong language. Words and expressions were being used to describe him like 'doesn't care'. Or, 'lazy'. Or, 'doesn't listen'. I mean, wow.

He immediately started telling me his reasons. I stopped him. I asked him how many CEO's the company had been through in his 3 years with the organization. He told me we were on our third in that time[11]. I asked him if the first two CEO's were bozos, incompetent or unworthy - no better than homeless people plucked off the street and given a corner office? Of course, he didn't believe that. Then I asked him if those CEO's, on the day they were removed from office, would have had 'reasons' for their troubles? The economy, an unworthy Board, a crumbling industry, poor talent in C-suite roles, etc. Don't give a shit, I told him. It happens. Good people get bad deals.

The question – the real question – is this: once your reasons start emerging (and they do for all people at all levels) what is your plan? How are you going to make it better? Why are *you* doing to overcome these obstacles? For some reason, people in these situations like to argue with me about fairness, as if I'll be struck by their logic and decide … what? I mean, what exactly is the end game? You are in trouble. You are not performing. You are not on the career track you want. Now,

---

[11] Completely true, by the way.

because of the *reasons* you're explaining to me, I'll come around and believe you're suddenly back on the CEO track?

When you're in trouble, don't fall back on your reasons. Lean on your *Plan*. What are you going to do that will radically change your situation? For example, if you *really* believe in yourself and you've been largely plagued by system errors, bad teams, warring departments, etc ... hey, maybe you can buckle down and fix those problems, pronto. And I mean *now*. But, if you're in situation where your credibility has taken a hit, where your usefulness has waned, where your star is diminished ... maybe it's time for a change? Maybe it's time to learn from this unfortunate experience, time to figure out how you'll grow from it and time to re-plant your career elsewhere. Demonstrate to that new organization how you faced your problems and how you've grown and changed.

No company gets to determine the value of *you*. Only you get to do that. But don't lean on your 'reasons' to help avoid the difficult work required to improve your situation. Either make the situation better or Get Out – those are your two choices.

CHAPTER THREE:
Externalities

The weather.

The bad boss.

The unproductive teammate.

The economy.

Inflation.

Bad budgets.

A bad team.

HR wasn't helpful.

Legal was too conservative.

Marketing wasn't aggressive enough.

Finance didn't support us.

The list of excuses goes on-and-on. All of them are what I call 'externalities', or things that have nothing to do with me. *I* didn't fail – everything and everybody else failed me. My idea and my leadership would have worked if not for all of them.

Guess what? I don't care about externalities. At the end of the day, fair or not, I put you in charge of the project. Did the project succeed? No. That's the first thing I need to know.

Beyond that, I just need to know one other thing: Do I believe in you? If I do, then this failure is just that – a failure, something to learn from. And, I want to see if you are taking the correct learnings from the failure. If it's marketing's fault, what did you not do to help marketing along and get their support? If it's a bad boss, what did you fail to do to get your boss's support, or how did you work with others to try to overcome this? In other words, because of this very expensive learning lesson you just got, how will *you* perform differently next time? I want to see that you are taking the right lessons away from this experience, and those lessons need to be about *you*, not your externalities.

Because, guess what? Externalities will be there next time, too, and the time after that. There are always forces at play that you can't control, especially in projects that are actually important to our company and to me[12]. I want to see that you recognize this and you've grown to account for externalities in your plan.

Additionally: When I see leaders who are consistently referring to externalities to rationalize & justify their lack of performance, this is a warning sign to me about not only the leader but the organization. If nobody is calling out this person on the accountability for their performance in spite of externalities, then the organization's chances are lessened.

Talking about externalities are like talking about farts – they're always going to happen and they're never beneficial to explore, so why bother mentioning them?

Do your job.

---

[12] See Chapter Twelve

CHAPTER FOUR:
Make Outlook Work For You

I think it's time for us all to admit it: We may be addicted to our calendars.

Is 'addicted' the wrong word? It's a heavy one, after all. But I've come to realize that I'm not that different from other professionals I work with, and all of us do pretty much whatever it is our calendars tell us to do. If Outlook or iCal tell us to go to a meeting, we go. If it says go to the dentist, we go. If it says make a phone call, we make it. How often have you excused yourself from a good, productive conversation you were having with a peer, colleague or team member just to run off to some meeting you didn't even want to be in? And why? Because our calendar said we had to go![13]

Let me pose this from a different perspective: Are you in a meeting *right now* that you don't think will do you or your business any good? Why are you there? Be honest! If you are being honest, it's probably because if it's on your calendar, it's bad form not to be there.

Sigh.

---

[13] With the advent of A.I. technology on our phones and watches (and in our ears!), it's only a matter of time before our calendars truly start talking to us. "You're fucking late, jackass!" is no more than 5 years away, right?

So, let's attack this calendar problem head-on. People have tried to be more aggressive with their schedules by rejecting meetings that they don't want to go to. This doesn't really work, because this is just an invitation for others to fill that time once they see you're 'available'. And, those declines become artillery for others to use when they want to show you're not being a team player.

So, really, what you need to do is feed your calendar with things that you *want* to do, so that when you look at that calendar you're being told to go places and do things that you really do want and need to do! In other words, if Outlook is currently feeding you junk food, schedule lots of healthy foods into your day!

But, what are health foods, in this case?[14] I break this down into four things:

1) **Boxes to be checked** – all of us have things to do. Our life is filled with lists of to-do's, and our careers are even worse. The problem is that, like eating junk food[15], checking off the boxes of things we need to do feels *too* good. If left to our druthers, we'd spend all day checking boxes and never feel anything but great about it! But, practically, very few of those boxes we check will be beneficial to our long-term strategies, our teams, our partners or our business. They're just things we need to get done as part of our jobs as execs – things like board slides, agendas for meetings, writing performance reviews and such. Busy work. Not that these things

---

[14] Uh, oh, I sense I'll be beating this potentially weak metaphor to death over the next few minutes. Hang with me.
[15] Yep, here we go!

don't need to get done, but just that they're not health foods – investments into the long term. I'll address how to stop yourself from checking boxes in the paragraphs below.

2) **Messages** that need to be delivered – Your team needs to hear from you. A lot. They need to be reminded about what's important to you right now and long-term[16]. They need help prioritizing. So, you have to talk to them, and spending all day in meetings and taking notes and such means you'll never get around to reminding them of what's on your mind, what's worrying you, etc. Talk to them, then talk again and again. Repeat yourself a lot.[17]

3) **Vision** that needs to be developed – You need to revisit what your short- and long-term vision is on a regular basis. Where is your team going? What's going to be important in six months, or a year? Are these things the same as what they were six months ago? Does your team know? Revisiting your vision is crucial for figuring out what messages you need to deliver to your teams (or partners) in #2, above.

4) **Careers** that need to be nurtured – Everything you're doing is built on the platform that is your career. Your career has different needs for healthy foods – it needs you to spend time with people who will influence your future roles and opportunities, to share with them what strategies you're working on, to seek their mentoring and more.

Okay, what do all of these four things have to do with your calendar? The reality is, all four should be *built into your

---

[16] See Chapter Eighteen

[17] But won't they hate me for this?, you ask? Sure, yeah, prob'ly.

schedule*! When you look at your calendar for the next one, two and three weeks, you should see items on that schedule that are related to all four of the above! Do you have time set aside to check boxes that need to be checked? Is it finite time, so you don't overdo it to the detriment of these other three things? Do you have time scheduled with your mentors? Do you have time set aside – ie, blocked – to wander around your team and ask them what they're working on and how it aligns to your priorities?

Feed your Outlook calendar with these items! Color code them so it's easy to see and distinguish between all four priorities when you're reviewing the next 3 weeks of schedule. If you're missing a color in those weeks, either talk to your admin about fixing your schedule or work out the next 3 months to make sure you're adding that activity back in.

Every Monday morning, block your first two hours of your day to review your calendar and nurture that calendar out over the next 3-6 weeks.

That way, when you're looking at tomorrow's schedule, you know you've spent time to ensure that there are some healthy calories built in.

CHAPTER FIVE:
Why Can't the Business and IT Get Along?

One of the assumptions I can make going into any company – big or small – is that IT and 'the business' don't get along very well. There will be sniping going on from both sides and the feelings are almost always personal in nature.

There are some root causes to all of this.

First, you need to understand the mentality of an IT team and organization. They're very arrogant. Now, that automatically sounds pretty mean and judge-y of me, but it's not intended to be[18]. It's a statement of observation intended to be useful for people who work with IT personnel in their jobs. And, it's largely true – they're arrogant.

Why? Remember, this is a group of people that has mostly spent its formative years solving problems. And, they're not just solving easy problems, they're solving problems with some real heft to them. How do we secure our environment from hackers? How do I find and fix the bug in my code? How do I optimize the website for mobile and desktop environments? How do I speed up our network connection to make a better user experience? How should we organize our data?

---

[18] This is the rare occasion when it's not intended to be, I realize. I am heavy "J" on the Myers-Briggs. This is shocking, I'm sure.

Not only that, but IT people are expected (above all other departments) to remain completely current on the latest developments in hardware, software, U/X and more. For as long as they can remember, people have been asking them questions from "How do I program the clock on my VCR?" to "How do I make all the apps on my phone stop wiggling?", and they're *supposed* to know the answers.

And, you know what – they frequently do!   They solve problems all the time! Far more often than they fail, our IT partners are successfully implementing tools, correcting problems and saving the company money. And that's the important note here: They have grown used to being correct, and they have grown used to being *asked* how to solve problems.

So, when they come face-to-face with real-life business problems outside of IT, they often break those problems down in a few predictable ways:

1) This problem has a root cause that is identifiable
2) This problem *can* be fixed
3) I'm a smart person with very well-developed instincts for how to solve problems
4) I would solve this problem faster than you if you'd just get out of the way and let me have the 'keyboard' (ie, control).

This thought process leads many IT people to offend their partners in other pyramids because they honestly believe that business people are bad at solving problems, have poor problem-solving disciplines and generally don't make decisions well.

They're usually wrong about this, but it's not coming from a terrible place.

Guess what, non-IT business people?   You're not so great yourselves.

First of all, more frequently than not you approach your IT partners without truly understanding your own problem.   I know the concept of the Magic IT Button that solves your technology problems is an old joke, but the truth is that most business teams still operate as if it exists.

One of the most common things you'll hear from an IT person is "Good Tech can't solve Bad Business Processes", and it's true. Broken processes permeate most large businesses and leaders truly hope that new technology will 'skip over' the efforts needed to correct bad procedures and get them directly to the answer.   Your sales team doesn't like to record its customer interactions into your CRM tool?   Well, then, the CRM tool isn't designed correctly! Or we chose the wrong vendor!   Or it's too slow on mobile devices! Or, whatever[19]!   Fix it!   But you can't expect these sales people to change their habits.

Second, business teams rarely even understand their own processes.   Things are not well documented or flow-charted in most companies, and the people in charge of projects often simplify their needs when talking to the IT teams assuming that fixes/corrections/upgrades will be possible once they see the new tool in action.   In other words, they want an iterative process, such as those used by operations teams to design processes in the first place (you never get it right the first time!).

---

[19] See Chapter Three on Externalities

Of course, in the technology world this thinking is expensive and inadvisable. My favorite analogy is this one:

> *'A project team describes everything they need to the engineers in order to build the perfect car, but are surprised when the first auto comes off the line and the steering wheel is housed in the trunk. They're outraged, but the engineers simply point to the requirements, which do not say that the wheel must be situated in the front seat ... or even what the business purpose of the steering wheel truly is! When the project team asks for fixes, they don't understand that you can't simply move the wheel back to the front seat – you have to change the transmission, re-calibrate brakes, re-test all of the safety features, etc.'*

This is not IT's fault. It's yours – every time.

How does this get better?

I can see three factors that will need to be improved in the coming decade:

First, leaders across the organization and project teams in particular need a type of (at least) remedial IT training to help familiarize themselves with how complex these systems have become in the modern age. For decades, leaders have been encouraged to get themselves at least a modicum of Finance training because of the crucial role that financial understanding plays in their success as leaders. Well, IT has reached that same resonance level for leaders, and it's time to just admit it.

Nobody is safe from the impact of technology on their businesses or careers.

Colleges, companies and other providers of education need to find ways to educate leaders-in-training on how projects work and how IT fits into project structure – everything from the need for security[20], the need for speed, the need to mitigate costs and everything that goes into achieving those goals. It's time to close this gap.

Two, I alluded to this earlier in the chapter, but your IT partners are not people you engage 'at the right time' in your project. They need to be partners the whole way through. Furthermore, they need to be *asked* what they think. Bring them not only onto the formal project team but *into the problem* – even if that includes getting them out to the field to see it for themselves. Embrace the challenges they may have for you that your processes need to be fixed as part of any solution. They will be important contributors and they will *save you money* in the long-term if you value their leadership and listen to their ideas.

Finally, at this point in the evolution of IT we need to acknowledge the 'arrogance' factor that I spoke to at the beginning of this chapter. It's not a shot at IT teams, it's a relevant character trait. Therefore, we need to begin addressing this in our development of IT teams the same way we might address other issues for leaders-in-training in other parts of the organization. Personality tests and other tools can be crucial to

---

[20] I know for a fact that most leaders think security is a big deal, but when it comes to *their* projects they underestimate how their decisions are impacting that security. They just don't understand how vulnerable many systems are.

making strong IT players at least self-aware, which is a crucial step toward making progress.

THOUGHTS ABOUT
CAREERS

CHAPTER SIX:

Return on Investment

I am frequently approached by mentees who are preparing for their Next Big Thing. They've polished their resume, they're on the job boards, they're hitting their networks[21]. In my eyes, most of these people are doing everything possible ... except, of course, for those things will actually be likely to land them the new gig.

I understand, that sounds mean and judge-y of me[22]. Let me explain. They're not wasting their time, per se, but they are stacking the odds against themselves. Why? First of all, most of the opportunities they really want are not on those job boards. The recruiters working most of the jobs you *could* be pursuing don't post their jobs on job boards, not even the big ones like Indeed.com. Why not? Well, companies of a certain size (think $20M to $1B) don't have fully dedicated recruiting staffs. They can't afford the time to do the posting and, if they could, the time it takes to whittle through the stacks of resumes they receive. No, they either work their own networks to find the people they hire or just directly hire outside recruiters who do the work for them.

So, what *should* you be doing? The answer is probably a question right back: What should you *have been* doing for

---

[21] A class five misdemeanor in twelve states.
[22] Or, I've said before, "That sounds exactly like me".

years now? That answer is networking, and much more broadly then you have been. I strongly recommend anybody reading this to read the book *Never Eat Alone*[ii].

Now, I want to address something much more profound than the networking part. And that is this: When you do get your chance to interview for that job, what are you going to say? Are you going to get the job? I sit in front of a lot of talented people who yearn for more scope and higher responsibilities – people looking for their first manager job, or maybe to reach the C-suite for the first time. They are very confident, but completely exposed. They talk about the challenge of getting people to recognize that they are 'ready' for these leaps. And, I think: That's right! You understand that the challenge is getting people to recognize that about you!

Remember, to a hiring manager, you represent a risk. Yes, a risk! And your job is not to explain to people why taking that risk is a good idea, it's to *reduce* that risk via the interview process. It's to explain how you are prepared for the role, are aware of the risks involved and have already put together a plan to mitigate those risks[23].

Are you ready for it?

---

[23] See Chapter Ten for a lot more on this.

CHAPTER SEVEN:

You're a Bozo

Do people like you?

Yeah, sure, some probably do. I mean, what are the odds that
all the people don't like you?[24]

I see a lot of executives (or execs-in-development) worry far too
much about the opposite question. "Are there people who
don't like me? If so, how do I turn that around?"
Unfortunately, the answer is the same – sure, almost definitely
there are people who don't like you! And, maybe you just
shouldn't be so worried about it.

The problem is that *most* people only get to form opinions on
you or your results through that narrow window of time in
which they're actually observing you. This is very different
from your boss or your team, who get to see you a lot. Those
people get very broad windows into your approach, your
intelligence, your strategy and more. They get a lot of data to
use in evaluating you. Some of those people will still
inevitably dislike you, and for *really* good reasons[25].
However, most of those people will come to like you. Unless
you are a complete fraud, most of what you do is actually pretty
good – that's how you go to middle management in the first

---

[24] 40% tops.
[25] You know what they are.

place! And most of them will lean on those accomplishments when evaluating you, such that their overall opinions will tend to vary between "pretty good" and "damn good".

This isn't true for people who aren't your boss, your team and a few choice comrades-in-arms. Most people in the company will only get small windows, and their evaluation will be based on what they see through those windows in the very short time span they're actually present and looking through those windows. While your overall competence means that they are *likely* to see you as a terrific teammate, on occasion there will be people (or groups of people) who are only looking out that window when you absent mindedly walk straight into a tree. You hit the tree, bounce backward, papers go flying and you fall to the ground in a puddle of mud. And, then, those people move along – they can't spend all day in front of your window.

That sucks! You are not a mud-puddler in general, but you're definitely a mud-puddler to the person who was watching at that moment. You're a bozo.

Now, if you happen to work long enough, the math just works out that in spite of your excellence many people will see you mud-puddling or hear about your mud-puddling. In fact, the higher up you go in business the more chances that all the people aware of you will break out into equal thirds in their opinions of you:

FIRST THIRD: You're a rock star. They would trust their children with you on a leaking boat in the Atlantic[26]. With you in charge, nothing can go wrong.

---

[26] Near, far, wherever you are …

SECOND THIRD: They're not sure yet.   They're still in the process of making up their minds about you.

FINAL THIRD: You're a bozo.

Alright, so I'm saying that a full third of people think you're not worth much.   Should you invest in this and try to fix the problem?   I would say, 'No'.   There are a third of people who already love you – make sure you're investing time in maintaining those relationships.   There's a second third of people who haven't made up their minds and can easily be swayed if they get to know you.   Find those people and invest. For the last third, the chances that you can *talk* your way out of the vivid visual they have of you in the mud is just, well, low. Maybe – maybe! – you'll get another chance when they walk by your window, and whatever it is you happen to be doing this time is enough to fully sway them back to 'Star' status.

But, probably not.   You only have so much time!   For every Bozo status you convert, you might likely be subjected to two more.   I'd rather invest my time on nurturing and sustaining my great relationships than worrying about the implications of a few less-than-ideal ones.

So, you're a Bozo!   Join the club.

CHAPTER EIGHT:

Networking for a Living

You don't have to be looking for a job to be networking. However, you *do* have to be networking to know if you should be looking for a job.

All jobs suck to at least some degree – that's why we get paid for doing them. So, if you're going to wait until you hate your job as the reason to look for a new role, then it will happen … but you'll never *really* know if the next job is worse than the one you're leaving!

Networking gives you access to information you need from outside the company to understand if you're sub-optimizing your situation. What do people make at other companies who do the work that you do? Recruiters, HR managers and potential employers will help you understand this. What are the expectations and opportunities of roles similar to yours but in other companies? Do they have more direct reports, broader scope, or vice-versa? Talking to people in your industry will help you learn this. What kind of benefits are your peers getting? What kind of promotions or pyramid changes might you be eligible for?

These are all things that networking will help you learn. Is your dream job sitting out there *right now* waiting for you to notice? By default, *not* networking will never give you the answer to that question.

At the very worst: Networking gives you the chance to say *no* to other jobs and to affirm that you are in exactly the right place at the right time for yourself.   You don't get that option when zero alternatives are being offered.

Showing up to your job tomorrow is indirectly saying 'No' to all the other opportunities that exist out there … whether you know they exist or not.   So, know what you're saying 'No' to, and to do that you need to talk to people.

Network!   It's not just for schmoozers.

CHAPTER NINE:

Salmon Swim Upstream, but Should You?

Salmon swim upstream to mate, a journey that kills many of them en-route and, once the act is completed, often kills the rest. I suppose some of them get eaten by bears, too.

Fun! Let's turn this into a business metaphor!

Let's say you're getting some tough feedback on your performance at work. I don't care if you're an analyst, a mid-manager or executive, the level doesn't matter. And, let's say it's clear from this performance feedback that your results either need to improve or your continued employment is jeopardized.

Fun again!

How do these two things correlate? Well, you have to understand that there are really three steps involved in turning around your performance.

- Step One is to **actually raise your performance** to meet the renewed/heightened expectations that have been placed upon you.
- Step Two is to **get your manager to agree** that you're meeting said expectations.
- Step Three is to **convince others that you're meeting these expectations**, because unless you get all the way to

accomplishing Step Three, your career is *at best* now reputationally stagnated at whatever role/position you currently hold. If people don't understand that you've improved sufficiently, they will not even consider you for promotions or laterals to new challenges within your company. And, if you're like me, the idea of spending the rest of your career in one job is very difficult to accept.

Getting to Step Three is going to be hard work – you will be the salmon swimming upstream. It's very possible you simply won't even make it upstream the entire way and you'll be let go en-route[27]. However, even if you do, the odds are increasingly strong that your best-case scenario is exhaustion at the mouth of the river. You got to Step Two and maybe even toyed with Step Three, but very little additional reward is likely.

Was it worth it?   Do you really want your career journey to be that of the salmon – hard work for little return?

Personally, I wonder if there is a different stream somewhere else that is offering better rewards for my exertion. Swimming is never easy, but another company will accept you as the person you *are* and will start by being excited to have you and your experience on-board. It's a fresh start with open opportunities for the future!   Your star can be re-born.

I'm not saying 'don't try' to turn things around, I'm saying be *conscious* of what you're facing. If you stay in your current role, you are committing (even if you don't consciously agree) to the three-step process I've laid out in this chapter.

---

[27] That's twice I've used that word in this chapter. That may or may not be impressive to you, but I will also remind you that I'm not sure I spelled it properly.

CHAPTER TEN:

Telling Your Story to Get Hired

Too many people go into the interview process without giving any thought to this question: "What is it going to take to get hired?"

Rather, people have become too well trained in the latest interview approaches, particularly 'SBO' or 'Situation/ Behavior / Outcome'. People are walking through the entire SBO interview process conscious of making sure they provide a complete answer using their experiences while providing all three elements of an answer (Situation, Behavior & Outcome) … but not making sure they are answering the core question of "What does this person need to know for me to be the person they hire?"

For example, let's say the interviewer asks: "Tell me about time when you solved a problem?" You respond: "Well, one time I was in a meeting taking notes when I dropped my pen. Without my pen, I could not take notes. So, I bent over and tried to find my pen. It turned out it had rolled out of reach. So, I took the person next to me as a partner and asked them if they could reach the pen. They could, and I was able to get back to taking notes."

Success! You have provided inputs that are necessary to satisfy the question and the SBO framework. Now, the more savvy interviewers amongst you readers will say, "interviewees need

to be trained to give role and experience-relevant answers" …
but that's my whole point!   Interviewees barely know how or
why the initial scenario I provided above isn't satisfactory.
They are so stressed out about the interview itself and about
making sure they cover all three elements of SBO that they
don't really stop to think about the more core issue – did their
answer get them closer to being hired?

Yes, they need to be trained!

Let's look at this from the perspective of graduating students:
for kids coming off campus, you have nothing to offer.   Just,
nothing.   You are awful interviewees.   I am both fortunate and
unfortunate enough to have literally done hundreds of on-
campus interviews in my life, looking for entry-level candidates
for the companies I worked for, and without exception I hated
every one of those interviews.

Undergraduate interviews are 100% about their sorority,
fraternity, group projects or some piddling job you held[28].
None of them tell me if you'll be a successful corporate
employee.   But, we ask you the "Tell me about a time …"
questions anyway, don't we?   Gah!   What are we really
looking to find out?

If you're a useless undergrad (and you are), really the only
things I can learn about you are:

---

[28] 100% of college campus interviews will contain one story about how they are
more responsible than their other frat/sorority mates, and 100% of all campus
interviews will tell a story about how one of the people in their Group Projects
for such-and-such class wasn't contributing his or her weight. It's just awful.
Get a fucking internship, kid. Or, rob a bank! Anything to tell me another
story.

1) Can you learn?
2) Are you smart? (Not the same thing as #1)
3) Are you accountable?
4) Will you work hard for me?

That's it! And, boy, I need all of those to be Yes! Beyond that, your grade-point average, personality and presentation will tell me the rest of what I can learn in our 30 minutes together.

So, formulate your answers to whatever stupid question I ask in an effort to answer those 4 question, above. "Tell me about a time you made a mistake?" This is about accountability, not about your ability to *avoid* mistakes! Learn that and understand it, and make sure your answer doesn't just tell me about a mistake, make sure it tells me about why you are accountable to the work you're assigned and are somebody with integrity!

That's what I really need to know.

Okay, now let's talk about qualified, executive-level applicants. You're up for a Director, VP or higher job. You've reached the executive ranks, which means your experiences and knowledge *should* be interesting to me as an interviewer. You should be able to tell some good stories. But, that doesn't absolve you from your ultimate mission – giving that interviewer what he/she needs to see you in the job.

Frankly, at this point in your life your problem is probably that you have too *many* stories and experiences. Which are those that will help you accomplish your goal (ie, getting hired for this job) the most?

Let's step back for a second, though, and answer a more important question: If this is truly your first entry into the executive ranks, are *any* of your experiences going to automatically portray you as qualified for these roles? The answer is mostly likely, 'No'.

There is an adage I shared in the book The Money Button that I'll share again here, and it was first told to me by a great mentor.

> *Brian, there's nothing about managing a group of 5 that tells me if you can manage 20 people.*
>
> *And there's nothing about managing 20 that tells me if you can manage 100.*
>
> *There's nothing about managing 100 people that tells me if you can successfully manage 1000.*
>
> *At some point, it's up to me to decide that you're ready and that I'm willing to find out with you.*
>
> *But, don't worry – if I'm wrong, we can always fire you later.*[29]

It's kind of a rough message, but it has an important theme – there are levels you will eventually get to in an organization where there really is no 'qualifying' you. You are a risky hire, no matter what. All you can do is try to convince the person that you are ready for the opportunity for everybody to find out together.

---

[29] See Chapter Fourteen about Compassionate Firing

How are some ways you can do that? Again, no matter what questions you get from the interviewer, these are some of the important messages you need to deliver:

1) No executive-level job can be properly defined in a job description. I will face a lot of non-prescribed problems and dilemmas if you give me this role. I have dealt with a lot of ambiguity in the roles I've held in my life. I'm comfortable with that and have an approach to it that will help me in this role.

2) My experiences have led me to this opportunity, not because I 'check all the boxes' (almost none of the candidates will be able to do so) but because I have been facing an increasing level of challenges along the way that have provided me with a framework for decisions making that I can describe and will follow.

3) I have a thick skin – I've faced a lot of scrutiny, questions and second-guessing in my life. That will only grow in this executive role. I'm ready for it.

4) There will be a number of years after I take this role where I'm learning from the fire hose. I have a strong group of mentors that I will be tapping into to help me understand the problems I'm facing, the mistakes I'm making and how normal all of this really is for executives going through the learning curve. Those mentors will be invaluable to me.

5) I'll accomplish nothing without a great team working for me, both directly and indirectly. I have clear experience hiring and firing to improve the talent around me, and I've made all the mistakes as a boss that you'd want me to have made prior to this job opportunity today, and will apply those learnings to great results in this new role.

So, in an interview I might ask you, "Tell me about a company-wide program you've led and the mistakes you've made." In that answer, I will be listening not only for what the project was about but for how you identified the people you hired to accomplish that program, who you asked for advice, who criticized you and how you handled that criticism (both proactively and in-the-moment), etc.

More than the specifics of the program itself, I need to know these things about you. Make sure you provide it to me.

Let's talk about the interviewers themselves. They are not nearly as prepared for these moments as they'd like to think, either.

At the end of the day, no matter what sort of lofty self-assessment you have of yourself, as an interviewer and hiring manager you're focused on these issues:

1) Will this person do a good job?
2) Will this person make me look good?
3) Will this person make me look bad?
4) Will this person need a lot of my time?
5) Does this hire add more risk to my portfolio of risks (business, career, job, etc.) or reduce that risk portfolio?

Notice that only one of those items is really about the job. The rest are personal and selfish, and I would argue against any person who suggests that these factors don't enter into their thinking. Oh, I highly doubt many of these interviewers are *consciously* asking these latter four questions – most people are simply not that self-aware – but it's always there.

So, as interviewers … is your interview process / questionnaire / profiling / whatever set up to answer these questions? Do you have something that you'll do in the 30-60 minutes you'll spend with the candidate that will address these concerns? If not, maybe you should?

THOUGHTS ABOUT
LEADERS

CHAPTER ELEVEN:
Sell the Vision

Tell, then do.

I have worked in the corporate world long enough to make it to the end of many projects[30]. But there is a lot of important work being done in corporate America outside of officially sanctioned projects. Every day, people are being developed, efficiencies are being created, teams are being restructured to handle new priorities, and more. Leaders of these efforts – often Manager and Director level – would like their teams to receive some credit for these advancements. It's usually a long wait.

Why? First of all, it can be difficult to trace the exact sources of progress. If you say, "We were only able to implement the new Marketing program this year because my team reprogrammed the system to allow personalized coupons," it sounds like you're suggesting that your team was uniquely integral to that result. But, your leaders are naturally oriented to assume you're overstating your role in that result and to downplay it. They're not being mean, just being human.

Second, if you don't champion your team's efforts, you're probably overestimating your leader's ability to 'connect the dots' on their own. You probably expect that your leader would hear about the personalized coupons program and say to

---

[30] Not without medication, but I'm still living!   Still living.

herself: "Hey, that must have involved my team! I should congratulate them!" Probably not going to happen[31]. And, if it does, your leader may consider it more of a 'following directions' effort on your part than a situation where you were driving innovation and strategy.

In other words, human people[32] are simply not great at connecting 'cause' and 'effect' on their own. It's not in our nature.

So, you need to reverse the order. Tell your leaders well in advance what it is you are planning to accomplish, and the value involved, and then go do it. This, in turn, comes back to your company's goal-setting process.

Almost all large companies have a goal setting process. But, let's be candid – these processes at most companies are usually pretty stupid. The process ultimately boils down to a list of things you already know you're tasked to do for the upcoming year – a to-do list. And, very likely, that to-do list is weighted very heavily toward the front half of the year, because (of course) that's the part of the upcoming year for which you have the best line-of-sight to what's coming.

To do the goal-setting process better, your goals should be aligned around strategic value that you're creating … and, optimally, those strategic values should be aligned to the company's goals. For example, if your company is trying to triple the growth of paper clip sales in the upcoming year[33], that should be your starting point. "How are *we* involved in

---

[31] Your leader should see Chapter Thirteen on Recognition.
[32] Which have to represent, what, at least 70% of your co-workers?
[33] No easy task. It's hard to beat Big Clip.

tripling paper clip sales?", should be the starting point for your goal-setting discussions with your boss and your team.

Let's say you're the head of procurement. Tripling the sales of paper clips would involve a lot of new product orders from your vendor – are they capable of delivering that increase in orders? Do you have the capacity in your supply chain needed to sustain the increased growth in orders from your customers? Can Accounts Payable keep up with the increased volume of purchase requisitions and payments needed to keep your vendors happy? Are there terms that need to be renegotiated in the event you're able to hit this goal (for example, could you get extra days before you have to make payments on your orders, or perhaps lower overall costs-per-unit)?

All of these are things in your control. Of course *you* understand that these things need to be done – this is your job and you're an expert at what you do. However, you can't forget that this also represents your contribution to the strategy of the company. As you build your goals, you need to energize not only your team but your leaders on the importance of these results. By calling out these connections in advance of the work involved, you are demonstrating your ability to see forward and anticipate obstacles, as well as to design a plan to deal with these issues and execute that plan.

It is important that you build this effort into your goals and share those goals with your leader(s) and partners early in the year. Remind them that your efforts are directly related to the ambitions of the company and must take priority. Make sure your goals are well understood. Ask them for their own goals to ensure they have anticipated what you're going to be doing and built those needs into their own plans for the year. For example, Accounts Payable should be telling you they are preparing for 'staffing up' in the event paper clip sales grow as anticipated. The Supply Chain leaders should be talking about re-organizing the slots in their warehouse in anticipation of the need for more day-to-day supply of paper clips.

Finally, you should build a process by which you check-in with your leader(s) and partners throughout the year to assess progress. Are paper clip sales meeting the ambition? What new challenges have come up? Is one group falling behind in meeting the new needs of the increased paper clip sales?

Notice that the point of this dialogue is not about how to best support increased paper clip sales. It's about you, and your ability to truly translate the importance of your work for your leadership team so they understand the value your team creates, even if you're not specifically driving a particular project.

This is not about taking credit. This is about the value of being recognized as a strategic leader, and the good ways you can put that recognition to work (adding resources, making new decisions for your department, etc.). You will have told your leaders up front what you're doing and why, which should naturally explain how you're prioritizing your efforts. You will have come back to your leaders throughout the year to remind them of what you prioritized and the progress you're making. And, when results occur, your leaders will naturally connect you to those results, because they've been hearing about your role all along the way. And, they will look to you for more leadership, ideas and strategy!

That's just the better way to do this, for both the company and yourself as a leader.

CHAPTER TWELVE:

What's a Business Decision?

In this book, you've heard me repeatedly discuss or reference the difficult nature of making business decisions[34]. It is what separates the very highest leaders from those who are still developing their careers. In fact, some day your ability to handle the stress and accountability of being a decision-maker will separate those who can go on to become c-suite level executives from those who will either not be chosen ... or those who will (wisely) choose to pull up short of those goals, because they do not truly want that pressure.

Real decision-making is not easy. You will never have enough data to know which direction to go. Decision-making for executives is always career threatening, but it also never stops. Second-guessing follows them everywhere.

However, one of the hardest things I've had to do in my career is to try to explain to ambitious career-building talent what a 'real' business decision is, and how it is still ahead of them in their careers. Here is an analogy I've learned to use:

> *Assume that you are walking down a path, behind*
> *which the path is on fire and will not allow you to*
> *retreat. There is simply no going backward. Ahead*
> *of you is a fork in the road.*

---

[34] Right? Hello? Are ... are you reading this thing?

Immediately down the left fork you see a hungry, angry bear. It repeatedly points directly at you and then its mouth to make sure you understand its intentions. To your surprise the bear has learned, against all odds, to vocalize the words "Human is food", though its diction is challenged because of the prolific drool coming out of its mouth.

Down the right fork are a series of stacked piles of $100 bills.

Technically, I understand you have a decision to make – left or right? The problem is this: when you, the candidate for my leadership role, want to impress me with your qualifications, you end up telling me stories that sound like the "bear vs. money" problem, where I admit you made a decision but it doesn't sound like a particularly difficult choice. My pre-teen kids would choose the 'money road' every time, so of course you did, too. I am not willing to pay much for that kind of experience.

Instead, now imagine that same situation: the path behind you is on fire, and you've arrived at a fork in the road. Down the left path you can see about 100 yards before the road simply disappears into a dark forest, into which you can see nothing ... but you do hear faint screaming. Down the right path you can see about 75 yards before the road bends and disappears over the horizon. In that same direction you can vaguely make out silhouettes against the setting sun that would appear to be flesh-eating monsters, but you can't be sure.

Neither road offers any detail about what challenges, problems or dilemmas exist beyond the immediate sight line.

You feel the singe of fire on the back of your neck as the road behind you is engulfed. Which path do you take?

Unfortunately, that's how most business decisions appear to executives – all the easy shit was already figured out by the people who work for them, so they're left with the *vampires vs. screaming noises* dilemmas. Your ability as my leadership candidate to relate circumstances that make you sound like an experienced decision maker in difficult situations like these makes you potentially valuable to me.

Before you get there, how do you learn how to handle *these* challenges? Experience! You learn, for example, to not walk these paths alone. Imagine the same scenario I described above, but now instead of finding yourself alone at the fork in the road, you have a team of leaders and mentors who have experiences different than your own. Some of them may even be able to say, "I once travelled 200 yards down the road to the left, and I can tell you that the first set of screaming is nothing to worry about." Yes, that information may not be enough to fully guide you ... but it's better than what you had before!

Ultimately, as an executive you will face very few risk-free situations. Those issues will rarely reach your desk. No, you're going to be stuck with the hard stuff from now on.

CHAPTER THIRTEEN:
Recognition

BREAKING NEWS – Recognition is important! Also, water!

But, how does recognition *matter*? A Harvard University study looked to explore this, and did three case studies.

In each of the three studies, they instructed students to perform a series of complex, but repetitive, tasks. The students would be compensated as they completed each assembly, and then asked upon completion if they'd like to continue along to another similar project for which they'd also be paid. They could continue to do the projects and be paid for as long as they were willing to do the work.

In the first study, when the students completed their projects and brought them for inspection, the instructor studied the final product, nodded and smiled approvingly, and said "Good job!" before asking the student if he wanted to continue. In this study, the students repeated the project more than 15 times before finally bowing out.

In the second study, when students completed their project and presented their work for inspection, the instructor did something quite startling – dropping any written work directly into a shredder without review and manually destroying any physical construction the student might have made right in front of his eyes. Not surprisingly, these students were less willing to work, repeating the project less than half as many times as in the positively-reinforced case. *This despite being paid exactly the same as the students in the first study.*

Most interesting was the third study. Here, students also completed their work and presented it for inspection. In this case the teacher (an actor) appeared meaningfully harried and distracted, and politely placed the students' completed work on the top of a very large pile that was obviously destined for some distant, future review. The teacher did say "Thank you" and asked the students nicely if they'd like to do another project. However, *the students in this case did not, on average, do any more work than the students in the second study*, in which the teacher actively destroyed the students' work in front of their eyes.

In some ways, I would suppose these results confirm what we already knew to be true - from a compensation standpoint, a little attention can often be more valuable than money. But, I would say this speaks to something larger than just the relationship between a manager and team member (or teacher and student). Every time you ask for a partner's help, or peer's, you have the same opportunity to show an interest in the final product. Remember that your inability to make time to ask questions, provide feedback or to do active listening can have much larger consequences than you might intend.

I also want to talk about four types of recognition that you have in your arsenal. So many people immediately associate 'recognition' with MONEY, which is Type #1. And, money is good. Nobody hates money. I could go into why money may be the least effective form of recognition in your arsenal, but you can find that in other books.

So, let's talk about other types of recognition. Type #2 would be the next most obvious form of recognition, which is THE STAGE. Whether we're talking about literally marching somebody up on a stage, or in front of a conference room filled with people, or putting their name 'up in lights' on message boards across the organization, there are some people who really, truly want this. And, for those people, give it to them. They believe that THE STAGE is correlated with their own ambitions and/or sense of security (they won't fire the person who was just employee of the month, right?). The stage works – use it liberally, but understand there are definitely people who *do not* want that.

Now we're getting into more obscure options for recognition. Type #3 is SCOPE. The idea here is that you are recognizing somebody's excellent performance by giving them more and harder types of assignments. Doing this is a signal of two important things (at least): 1) that we are plainly testing this individual for their ability to do harder work, a signal of possible future promotion, and 2) a chance to do harder work with more risk and more difficult decision-making, which is *truly* the most important developmental growth you can give to somebody. So, SCOPE is a great option. Just make sure you're walking through with the employee how this extra work is about recognition – don't leave it to them to wonder, as they could end up thinking it's just punishment for being good.

Finally, the most non-obviously form of recognition that probably matters the most when it comes to this portfolio: Type #4 is TIME. Your time as a Director, Vice President or C-Suite employee is the most precious commodity you have. Your team knows that. Therefore, if you ask an employee to spend some of that time with you, they will universally understand that this is important, valuable and meaningful. That TIME can be used simply to listen to them recap the work they've completed, or to have them describe the project they're about to take on. Even more valuable is if you use that TIME to ask them questions about the business, the team, the problem at-hand, or otherwise. "What do you think we should do?" Gives that employee the impression that you not only care about their opinion, but that you took the time to solicit it. Ask follow-up questions. Challenge their thinking. Share your own thoughts, which they will love to hear. But making the time for your most valuable and developing team members is almost the most singularly personal valuable choice you can make from this list.

One last thought to augment this: Think back to the last time YOUR boss cancelled a regular status on you. How did that make you feel? Even if it gave you time back in your day, even if your boss is an unrelenting jerk … I'm pretty sure that in your heart-of-hearts you recognized it as a lost opportunity. That's how your team feels about you! TIME – think about it!

CHAPTER FOURTEEN:
Compassionate Firing

The below script could be a valuable message for you to memorize in one form or another:

> *I want to talk to you today about your performance. It's not where I would have hoped it would be by this time in your role.*
>
> *If you're satisfied with your performance, then I've done a bad job explaining the expectations of the role. That's on me – I need to learn from that and grow as a leader.*
>
> *But I'm not going to let my mistake be compounded by another mistake. So, starting today, I'm going to work to make sure those expectations for you and this job are crystal clear. That's why I've written this information down and am handing it across to you now. I based these expectations on the job description I initially wrote for your role, though I've made some tweaks to account for how this job, like all professional roles, have evolved since you were hired.*
>
> *Note that these are the *baseline* expectations for the job. In other words, doing what's written here is my minimum expectations for your performance*

going forward. Accomplishing some of these items, but not others, is not a passing grade.

This is going to be a challenge for you. I am not the only person who's recognized that your performance hasn't been where we'd like it to be. So, you not only have to raise your performance in the coming weeks, but *if* you do that, you and I will need to work to ensure that others are seeing that improved performance ... not just me.

I know you have ambitions in your career that go beyond this role. To achieve those ambitions, you are not only going to have to raise your performance, you're going to have to re-establish your reputation in a way that opens those opportunities for you. That's another challenge: Are you willing to commit to not only the effort to raise your performance, but to also work with other leaders, peers and your team to rebuild that reputation? All of that is going to take time – it will slow your progress toward your ambition. That's just a fact.

I realize you may not agree with the assessment I'm making, nor the reputation that exists of you in this company. I appreciate that – I want you to be aggressive and to have a high sense of what you bring to the table. However, it's simply a fact here that I'm not seeing the performance *I* want. So you're going to have to make an important decision on whether continuing at this company is your best path to meet your career ambitions, and whether *it's worth the increased time & effort you'll need to deploy just to get back on-track in your job, much less for the career you want to build. If you believe we're wrong in our assessment, another company may be the best fit for you. That's your decision to make.*

If you do decide to stay with us and attack this uphill challenge, then I'm with you. I will walk you through the expectations on this list line-by-line and make sure we're aligned with not only what these baseline expectations are, but what excellent performance would look like to me (which, again, goes *beyond* the baseline expectations I've compiled for you on the list). I owe you all of that. Then we'll work on a weekly plan to review your performance and help you get back on track.

However, I want to be sure you understand this: There is a timeline. Within 45 days, if I'm not seeing the progress I'd like, this whole process will get more formal and I'll work with HR to introduce a PIP, or Personal Improvement Plan, into the mix. That process will have its own sixty-day (or less) timeline for your improvement and could end with termination if you're continuing to miss the expectations. I owe it to you now to explain that. We're not going to persist at these levels of your performance.

Do you have any questions on what I'm saying? Do you understand that I have to have a timeline for this process to see improvement, both for your sake and mine?

Thanks. We'll talk again at the end of the week to go into detail on what's next.

[Then, leave. Let them think. There will be a lot of emotions involved, and that's okay, too. You need to help them make the decision to stay or leave, and then to understand the process forward. Some people *will* improve, and that's terrific, but others will not and you must act.]

I believe the script above gets that process going for you as quickly and humanely as possible, and treats people as professionals. They *can* have a different take on the situation than you. Than *can* believe they are better than you're making them out to be. I actually appreciate this! But, if that's the case, they are not likely to believe raising their performance is necessary, in which case you need to introduce the idea of changing companies as an approach for them. You have to make it clear that anything other than improvements are not going to be acceptable *here*.

One last thing – be prepared if the person makes a quick decision that exiting the company is the right course of action for themselves. If so, make sure they hear you say that you will give them time to execute their search, but that, too, has to have a timeline associated with it before you'd expect their resignation. Ninety days is usually fair and sufficient for their needs.

CHAPTER FIFTEEN:

Attack the Elephant

You're in the room, pitching your idea. This is the moment. And, unfortunately, you're sharing the space with the proverbial elephant.

You know the elephant – it's the thing that everybody sees in the room but nobody is talking about. It's the distraction. By definition, it's not helping you.

In your case, the elephant could be many things:

- The leader who's looking at you, thinking 'You failed the last time you were given a similar chance that you're asking for now'
- The fact that there is no money left in the budget
- The reality that there is somebody in the room who doesn't like you or your ideas
- Your knowledge that the people you're talking to heard a similar idea recently and vociferously rejected it
- The reality that your idea is the opposite of what management just said it wants people to focus on

Whatever it is, talk about it. Not only that, but be the *first* to talk about it. Bring it up aggressively and get it on the table. Talk about that thing – whatever it is – before anybody else gets an angle on your elephant. It's yours – own it and tame it.

"Look," you'll say. "What I'm about to say will not be appreciated. The last time I brought this up you were all very upset at the suggestion. Here's why I'm bringing it up again."

Ignoring the elephant during this meeting / presentation / pitch / performance review is to your detriment. Addressing it shows the team that you understand the controversy and its implications and that you're prepared (or preparing) to address them.

Don't be afraid of elephants – they just need to be fed.

CHAPTER SIXTEEN:
The Butler Did It

I'm going to share a murder mystery with you.

First of all, I want you to know that the butler is the murderer.

Wait, whoops! Did I just spoil the story? Don't worry – this is a business presentation. Spoiling the story is not only the point, but I would argue that you need to do it fast as possible.

Meetings take too long and people's attention spans are shortening. In spite of this, too many people are still telling linear stories when they present to management. They learned this process too well during their years in K-12 school and it's been reinforced with every novel they've read since. But it's the wrong approach in a business setting.

Let me challenge you this way: Can you tell me the reason I should listen to you within the first 15 seconds of the meeting?

"Because of growth in electrical rates, we are going to see utility costs grow four times faster than sales over the next five years."

"I think we can cut our payroll costs by a third over the next three years, but I don't think you'll like the idea because it changes how we run our checkout lanes."

"Our data says we're not developing enough leadership talent within our HR Organization, and I'm here today to get your ideas on how to fix it."

"We cannot afford the important training programs we're currently running and Finance is threatening to cut it. We also know we can't afford to cut the programs due to the impact it will have on customer service. So, I need ideas on how to get that training implemented for one-third of what we're spending today or we'll lose our ability to make this decision for ourselves."

Direct. Punchy. Tells people right away if your problem is important enough for their attention.

The other benefit: You'll find you can now tell the story (and present the data) that supports your opening statement in a much faster fashion than if you'd tried to tell the story in a linear way. When you tell a story like a novel, it's hard to skip chapters because there are important characters and clues to carefully unravel for the audience, clues that support the surprise at the end of the book. When you just tell people right away who the murderer is, you can avoid all of the background except that which directly supports the outcome. All of this helps your meeting go faster and for collaboration to begin earlier.

It's business, not bedtime. Skip as many chapters as you can and get on with it.

CHAPTER SEVENTEEN:

How to Get Rid of Your Worst Good Idea

Bad ideas aren't a big problem for most leaders. Too many good ideas are.

People look up to leaders and think, "The challenge of being a leader is to sort out the good ideas from the bad ones." Not true. The bad ideas get identified very quickly and thrown out. The problem is the exact opposite – people are constantly bringing you good ideas and they don't understand why you won't act on them.

They don't understand that good ideas fall from the sky. HR wants to tweak the performance review process to put more of an emphasis on manager-team member conversation. An analyst has an idea for cutting hours in the plant by 1%. The CEO wants you to work on his "ACME, Inc. 2.0" initiative.

I wish the issue was that these were all bad ideas! They're not. All of these probably have some semblance of a positive ROI[35] associated with them. And, that's what makes people shocked when you won't undertake their project!

So, the issue is this: How do I get rid of the 'worst good ideas' that are in my portfolio, the ones that will distract me from accomplishing the biggest goals I have for my team or the company?

---

[35] Return on Investment

Simple – you need to do a better job of communicating.

Your job as a leader is to communicate to your team, your partners and your boss on those things that are your most valuable goals for the coming year, and why. That explanation should also help people understand how you're aligning your resources to those goals – in other words, which projects are getting your best people? Where is your budgeted spending going? What capital do you need to create that result?

If you do this successfully, you will find that you now have the makings of a list that you can share with people when they bring you new 'worst good ideas'. Rather than arguing against their idea, which always feels somewhat personal and like pushing water uphill (they will have a response for every argument you make), you are arguing for what you *are* investing your time to accomplish.

In other words: "Billy[36], I'm not avoiding your idea. It's a good idea. But, first, I must accomplish these five very large deliverables I have for the year, which are crucial to our strategy as a company. I can take on more projects when these things are done, but they're not done yet. And that's why your idea has to stay on the shelf for now."

---

[36] If the person's name is not Billy, you should of course substitute their name here. Unless you don't have any patience for names, in which case 'Billy' will do fine and sends its own messages which 'Billy' will surely not miss.

CHAPTER EIGHTEEN:
Describing Disney Land

One of the most important actions you can do for your team as the leader is to formulate your vision. What is it that you're asking the team to do?

A lot of leaders think they're doing this by saying things like "make profit" or "serve the customer". It's not enough. There is a lot of detail in a good vision that's missing. I call this "describing Disney Land".

Said differently, it's not even enough to tell your team "I want you to make a Disney Land for me." Sure, it *sounds* like direction for your team, but there's a lot missing in that statement!

For example:

-   I love roller coasters. There should be several roller coasters as part of our new Disney Land.
-   Some of the roller coasters should be good for little kids and some for thrill seekers.
-   We want this place clean – there should be waste baskets every 100 feet for people to drop off their garbage, or (being the disgusting human beings they are) people will litter.
-   We want lots of clean, accessible bathroom options for families.

- We charge an overall fee to get into the park, not individual tickets. So we don't need facilities (or personnel, or training) for ticket purchasing or ticket-taking.
- Disney Land should be fun – our employees should be smiling all the time to set that tone.
- People will come to celebrate Disney Land because of the wealth of characters we will tap into from across the Disney Universe – princesses, cartoon characters and more. These characters should be everywhere – walking on the sidewalks, in pictures, on t-shirts and more.

And on and on. Note that nothing I have to say above describes exactly how much money you want to make or what sales should be. Those are outcomes, but they're not controllable. If the outcome of your venture isn't 'profit', then you either had a poor vision or you didn't execute it very well.

Don't let it be that second one. Describe the components of your vision carefully to each and every employee you have and help them understand *their specific role* in delivering you to that vision. The rest takes care of itself. And, better still, you'll find you have more engaged and long-lasting employees – they know exactly why they are part of the team and how they are doing, even before you tell them (are the bathrooms clean? If not, that's my fault!)

CHAPTER NINETEEN:
How E-Mails Change

You get an e-mail from the SVP of Marketing. "What assumptions did we use for inflation in our 2019 budget?"

Your stomach sinks. There is no easy answer to that question. So you begin:

> *"Well, it's complicated. There were seven different inflation assumptions used to build the 2019 budgets in Marketing. For payroll we used 2.5%, but that only starts in July when we give out promotions. We also held back 1% for promotions on top of that 2.5% number, so it weights out to 2.7%, really. Then, we used 5% for paper cost increases because that's been the average for the last 3 years, but then Finance had to cut our budgets to hit our number so we only put in 3%, so it really depends on if you want to know what we're assuming (which would be the 5%) or what we're actually budgeted to do (3%). To get to the 3%, I know your team is trying to use slightly less recycled paper, which costs more than standard paper, for the ads. They're also cutting 4 pages out of 3 different weekly ads this year. Another inflation number is in the costs for our External Resources, which we put at 0% this year because we're going to competitive bid this out ..."*

And on and on it goes. Because you've got to explain, right? That leader *needs* to know!

Then you get a response back from the SVP saying: "I just wanted to know how much our overall budget grew over LY's results."

And you respond:

> *"We grew 6% over last year in our budgets this year. Note that this includes $265k of costs related to your taking over the Internal Communications team, which was in HR last year and is now in Marketing. If you didn't have Internal Communications you would only be up 2.5% over LY. Note that we've overspent our budget by 6% year-to-date, so the 6% increase year-over-year may still turn out to be accurate, even when you eliminate the Internal Comm team."*

And you get back from the SVP: "Thanks". But you suspect they don't really mean it.

Pay attention to this trend. For every level higher than you in the organization do you notice that the messages get shorter? One sentence, two maybe. They don't have time to write. So, do they have time to read?

Instead, maybe this exchange would prove beneficial for you:

> *SVP: What assumptions did we use for inflation in our 2019 budget?*
>
> *YOU: That's a loaded question and I'll bore you to death with details. **Why don't you tell me what***

question you've been asked and I'll give you the quick answer.

SVP: I'm filling out a form for Nielsen and they're asking how much our company's ad budget is growing year-over-year. Keep it simple.

YOU: Ah. You should say 3% - it's really 6%, but that includes expenses you took in 2019 that were part of HR last year.

SVP: Thanks – I agree with using 3%.

Anytime 'it's complicated', ask a question back *quickly* rather than stewing over the answer. It's probably less complicated than you think, and they don't have time for rambling. Eventually, you'll learn to talk *and* ask questions like an executive, a good thing to learn.

THOUGHTS ABOUT
IMPROVEMENT

CHAPTER TWENTY:
Building on a Rickety Platform

If your company is old enough (let's say, 30 years or more), you've got problems with legacy systems. I don't even have to ask.

Legacy systems are those things that were built far enough back that 1) there aren't many people who understand them anymore, 2) they severely limit what you're able to actually do as a company, and 3) they're so intertwined with other systems that replacing them is not just difficult but precarious.

So, you just kind of keep building around them.

I'm from Minnesota[37], so my analogy sounds like this:

> *Imagine some guy named Steve goes out into the middle of a frozen lake and builds an ice house. Now, 'ice house' may be a bit of a stretch for this structure. It's more of a lean-to, some plywood nailed together into a box. It's not a terrible box — it does lean in different directions based on the wind*

---

[37] Official State Motto: *At least we're better than North Dakota, South Dakota, Iowa, Nebraska and most of Canada. Sure, we can't hang with Quebec, but they've got that French thing going on, which doesn't seem really fair. Anyway, this Motto is beginning to run on, so we'll talk to you later. Love, Minnesota.*

– but it keeps Steve warm enough when he wants to fish.

Later, some well-intended new leaders come out on the lake and see what Steve has done. They're under pressure to deliver more than just fish, and to do it quickly. They have ambitions and they have ideas. They're very smart, and it's reflected in their goals. They don't have time to replace what Steve did, so they just start by building on top of his little shack, a 'second floor' to the ice house, if you will. It works, it's fine.

In fact, this second floor is even pretty nice. They took the time to paint those walls and install some heating. Of course, this isn't the best idea for a house whose very foundations are ice and whose first floor sways with the prevailing wind ... but for the people on the second floor, it's pretty exciting.

Throughout all of this, Steve is downstairs and he's just annoyed. He keeps fishing like he always did – to him, that's what this building was built to do, and nothing else.

But, then, through no fault of their own, those new leaders end up getting replaced, and before you know it Steve's looking at even newer people who are talking about adding a *third* floor to his shack. These guys spent some time on the second floor, and while they agree it was 'nice' it's not what they see for the long-term. So, they build a much larger unit right up on top, except this time they really do it up. It has bathrooms (don't ask!), wi-fi and more. Everybody who visits the third floor agrees it is exquisite.

The one thing they do note, however, is that every so often there is a discernible scent of fish that wafts throughout the whole unit. Now, the people on the second floor (those who were left behind when the first set of new leaders came along) know this just means Steve must be visiting and that he clearly scored a few fresh fish which he's cooking up for lunch. They've been dealing with the 'Steve issue' for some time, installing some extra insulation in the walls and floors and bringing in some scented candles for just the right moments. Note that they haven't actually changed what Steve is doing, they're just doing their best to work around it. But for the people on the third floor, the whole thing is a complete mystery, and as they can't understand the root cause they are clueless as to what action to take.

Steve, meanwhile, is planning no changes to his routine. In his mind, this ice-house was intended for one purpose: Steve's fishing. He sees nothing wrong with that purpose and isn't motivated to change, even when one of those idiots on the second floor comes down and asks him for ideas about how to remove the fish smells. They can ask all they want, but in Steve's mind they shouldn't have built the second floor in the first place (much less the third), so why is any of this his problem? Steve also wonders if anybody else hears the cracking in the ice, a sound which is definitely much louder since

*the third floor was built. He also wonders if
anybody has a plan for when Spring thaw comes.
But, he shrugs that off because he'll be long gone
before that happens.*

How many of you work for companies where you're working
each day on top of Steve's little shack? Can you feel the
swaying anytime a sharp wind hits the lake? I love-love-love
ambition and new ideas, but ultimately when you realize you
have an infrastructure problem that's getting in the way of those
ambitions, you have a choice to make – either start a new build
off to the side of what you've already done, or attack the
infrastructure itself.

Stop trying to work around the fish smell[38]. In fact, that smell
is probably a sign of something much worse to worry about (ie,
the Spring Thaw).

It's crazy how risk averse people are in everyday management
of the company, but how willing they are to endure these nutty
risks with their infrastructure.

---

[38] This was *almost* the state motto of Minnesota.

CHAPTER TWENTY-ONE:
You Got the Problems Wrong

"You solving all the problems?"

This is one of those glib comments people throw at you as they're passing you in the hallway. It's another version of "You working hard or hardly working?", "What do you know today?" or "Watch where you're swinging that axe, jerk!"[39]

However, unlike most of these other comments, the first one gets me thinking. Am I solving *any* of the problems? I mean, I'm busy as shit. As an executive, I've got all kinds of things I'm tasked with doing, and my hours couldn't be worse. But what am I accomplishing? I'm getting Board presentations ready. I've got a new forecast submitted. I got all of my annual reviews sent to HR for processing before the deadline. These are the things I get reminded of if I don't get them accomplished.

But the *actual* problems? I've got systems that absolutely will not work for the new product line we're rolling out. I can't trust the data on the reports I'm using to make decisions. I can't keep the pipeline of talent full enough to replace all the great people we're losing thru attrition, most of them simply because they're getting offered more money for the same jobs (which doesn't speak well of our company on multiple levels).

---

[39] Grrr, Mondays!

So, what did I do today? Again, I was busy. I got all kinds of things done, and people praised that output. I went straight to bed when I got home, I was so tired after it was done. But tomorrow I will have the same *real* problems.

So, now when somebody asks "You solving all the problems?", I answer: "Yep, but it turns out we might have gotten the problems wrong!"

What about your company – are you working on the right problems?

CHAPTER TWENTY-TWO:
Learning Models

As the years go by, companies are learning more-and-more about effective change management practices. A lot of change management comes down to solid communication and good training.

But what is 'good training'? A lot of people who roll-out new tools and products in their companies get frustrated by their training teams when the end-users do not successfully adopt the new technology. But, maybe the trainers were actually set up to fail?

I compare technologies in my mind using this framework: Was this tool built according to the Microsoft expectations for learning or the Apple approach to learning?

The Microsoft approach is to build technology that is powerful and useful in many different ways ... but has a rather large learning curve. Microsoft Excel has boundless utility – you can make it do so, so many things. However, you have to actually learn a lot about Excel to even get it to do *anything*. You have to learn how to build formulas, manipulate cells, use the toolbars, trouble-shoot errors, format, save files, and more. There is a long learning curve from when you *first* start trying to learn Excel until you feel competent enough to use it at all. That's why so many people give up in frustration.

The Apple approach is the opposite. Apple's technology, particularly its phones and iPads, are built with extremely limited utility but with rapid adoption in-mind. They take away your power to manipulate the tool, but in turn give you an ability to use it and feel successful right away.

Let's use an example: I want to build a tool for calculating home mortgage payments. To build such a calculator in Excel, I need to learn a lot about Excel itself before I can start. It might take a few days (or longer) to get up to speed. However, once I've accomplished this goal, I can probably further adapt the home mortgage calculator into a car payment calculator in no time at all. I have *earned* the knowledge necessary to do this adaptation via my days of study.

To build that same calculator with Apple technology … well, I just wouldn't. I could probably just buy an iPhone, open the box, turn it on, download an app for home mortgages and be to calculating my payments inside of 15 minutes. However, I would have *zero* capability to convert that app into a car payment calculator – it's a fixed-function app. On the flip side, I could just download a car payment app to solve that problem. Now I've learned two things!

Excel is designed to reward people who invest the time into learning a capability. Apple is built to provide limited but rapid successes.

Over time, the two different approaches to design start to overlap like the chart below, with Apple providing lots of quick wins to its user base that teach them how to solve problems without learning much. Microsoft requires renewed re-investment to grow your ability to solve problems. I'm not arguing that, over the course of time, either one is a best way to gain knowledge and capabilities. It's just two different ways.

CHART 22.1

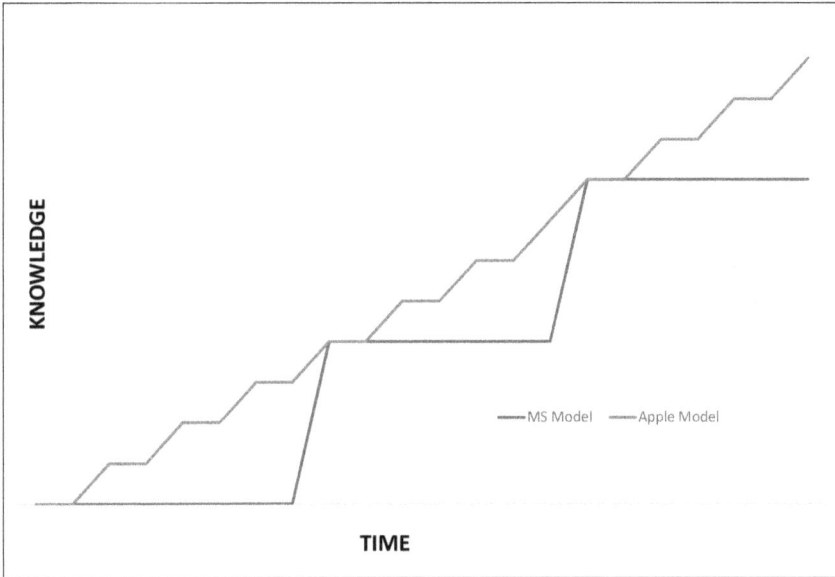

Now, let's put this in the context of your business goals. **If you are trying to design a tool that will adopted as fast as possible by the most end-users**, building tools the Apple way seems like the way to go. Your tool should be built with less power and flexibility, and instead focus on a simple interface designed to achieve ruthlessly finite goals.

If your tool simply *must* be more complex, then you should build your training plan understanding that you must invest the time and encouragement to users required to get them to their 'first wins', which are farther down the road. You have to keep bringing them back and encouraging the investment they are making.

Understand this before you begin the development process, not just before the training has to begin.

CHAPTER TWENTY-THREE:
Anti-Fragility

There is a concept created and developed by acclaimed author Nicolas Taleb in his book *Anti-Fragile: Things that Gain from Disorder*[iii]. It is an exceptional book and I highly recommend it for evolving your thinking about your business and business life in general.

I will cite directly from Mr. Taleb to define Anti-Fragility:

> *Anything that has more upside than downside from random events (or certain shocks) is anti-fragile.*

To differentiate the 'fragile' from the 'anti-fragile', Mr. Taleb goes on to say:

> *The 'fragilista' belongs to that category of persons ... who often defaults to thinking that anything he doesn't see is not there, and what he doesn't believe does not exist. At the core, he tends to mistake the unknown for the non-existent ... he believes the reasons for things are automatically accessible to him ... when you are fragile, you depend on things to follow the exact planned course with as little deviation as possible.*

I am going to argue that companies across America – big, small, private, public – are 'fragilistas' in Mr. Taleb's parlance. They either outright believe that things can be under their control or operate as if it is true. Every budget process in every headquarters across corporate America is based on this principle – that things are predictable and largely under our control. This is *not* bad, and not even Taleb argues that it is bad – it is simply pointed out.

The question you should be asking yourself is – why am *I*, the author, bothering to point this out[40]? Because when you operate your business as if you understand how things are supposed to work, and as if you understand what could possibly happen to your business and how you would respond, you are taking wild risks. Essentially you are operating a fragile business, one where if that thinking is in any way proven to be non-true, most likely through shocks due to the economy or changes in competition, you risk losing everything much more suddenly than you might expect. This is not to suggest that such shocks are *going* to happen, simply that there is no real way for you as a leader of your business to know that they won't happen.

Therefore, the encouragement is to **balance your portfolio with risks and investments that have an ability to turn an upside – and, in particular, a *very* large upside – in the case of such shocks.** These anti-fragile investments do not have to be

---

[40] Good question. My publisher does have a required word count before I can submit this book and be paid, after all – I could simply be stalling for time. And what a *time-honored* action that is, stalling for time. I could take you back to the ancient Greeks, who perfected the form with their development of governing bodies across their nation-states, but to do so would be beyond the word count the publisher is allowing me to put in footnotes, so go ahead and look that one up for yourselves.

outside your industry … though they may cause you to redefine where your industry begins and ends.

This is where innovators and disrupters are critical to your business model. If you ask most of your current leaders where you should invest, you will understandably be barraged with ideas that go toward mitigating the known risks and challenges or your organization. You will get almost no responses to this question that ask: What if our business <u>has</u> to change? Where does explosive upside exist that we're not yet tapping, and do we have access to those returns should they become viable?

CHAPTER TWENTY-FOUR:
Free Money Fridays

This is an exercise I like to do in large groups to show them the futility of 'Change Management'.

First, I have a person come up to the front of the room with me. That person is told they are one of my Brightest and Up-And-Coming Stars of the organization. Because of this, I am giving them a great project to build their reputation, something that will have great results for the company and its employees while not being that difficult to pull off.

I call it Free Money Friday.

The idea behind Free Money Friday is that every Friday all of the employees of the company will get a bag of free money as a way of driving engagement. The bags will be left out in the cafeteria each week by lunch time on Fridays for people to pick up. I figure the rest of the details will take care of themselves and wish the employee luck on implementing this policy.

After I sit down and leave the details to my Executive-in-Training, a line of audience members stands up to read from cue cards I've given them. My Up-And-Comer needs to respond to this feedback successfully to prove to me his continuing worth.

Here are the cue cards the audience has been given:

1. *"In my bag of money last week, there were $50 and $100 bills. Nobody takes those bills except the*

bank. *Can't you just put in more 5's and 10's so I can just use the cash without going to the bank?"*

2. *"Are you withholding separate money each week outside of what's in the bag to pay our taxes? Or, am I just supposed to know how much of the bag-of-money not to spend?"*

3. *"The bags of money you're giving us have a big dollar sign on the outside of them, like they used to show in old Bugs Bunny cartoons. On Fridays I have to stop twice to pick up my kinds on the way home, and I get nervous leaving that bag sitting in the car. What should I do to prevent theft?"*

4. *"In last week's bag, there were a lot of $5 and $10 bills. That's a lot more for me to have to sort and organize when I go to the bank and deposit it. Nobody uses cash anymore – can't you just put larger bills in the bag to make this easier?"*

5. *"I have worked at this company for 20 years. Why do the new people get the same size bag of money as me?"*

6. *"I work in procurement. There is no money in my budget to pay for Money Bags to hold all this money, or for anybody to go to the bank to pick up the money you need for stuffing into bags. What are you going to do?"*

7. *"I work in the St. Paul building. Do I really have to drive over to the Minneapolis building every Friday just to pick up my Bag of Money?"*

8. *"I cut my hand on the crisp dollar bills you're putting in these bags. Do I have to pay for the*

bandage for my hand out of my own bag money, or
will the company cover that separately?"

There are no ways to mitigate all of these concerns. People are selfish and self-centered and will always be so[41]. Change Managers who proscribe to endless cycles of documenting the needs of every audience will make all of this clearer, but they will *not* eliminate the inconsistencies that exist across people and teams.

That doesn't mean you shouldn't do your homework as a Change leader. It means that sometimes feedback is inevitable even in what appear to be the best of circumstances, but that doesn't mean you shouldn't make the intended change.

Have conviction in your ideas and execute them soundly. And, then, expect people to behave as people!

---

[41] See "The Money Button" on Amazon.com today!

THOUGHTS ABOUT
HOW THINGS
ARE
CHANGING

CHAPTER TWENTY-FIVE:
Things I Don't Think Will Survive

It's getting harder to cut costs. As corporations, we've been through so many cycles of cost-cutting and fat-trimming that by necessity too many companies are starting near the bone whenever they go back to the P&L to solve short-term earnings problems.

These days, when you go to the HR, Finance and IT teams for cost savings you need to understand that what you're really asking them to do is to kill the sacred cows. You know what these are – things that you do because you've always done them. They're the processes that make you feel like a big corporation.

There are three expensive functions that I think will not make it through the next 15 years at major companies.

Budgeting:

Imagine that you're holding a capital/resource allocation meeting in your company[42], and an aspiring leader steps up to the panel and gives you this doozy of a project request:

> *"I would like to receive $20M and more than 25 full time headcount to run a process that I'm going to call 'budgeting'. In this process, I will run*

---

[42] Worst. Fantasy. Ever.

intensive bottoms-up spreadsheet exercises to build our financial plan for the coming year."

"That sounds amazing!" you say. "So, these exercises will use forward-looking expert opinions on wage growth, inflation, job market changes, interest rates and the like to project key assumptions for our business?"

"No, not at all. We basically have a guy named Steve[43] in FP&A who makes reasonable guesses on those things and, if we're lucky, shares those guesses consistently across all of the people involved in the process."

"Okay," you say. "But, these spreadsheets will find a way to hold our teams accountable for performance and improvement?"

"Absolutely, so long as the performance and improvement you're looking for was already in our financials last year, because LY will be the basis for every calculation we do, without exception."

"Will the rollups be valid and useful?" you ask.

"Not even remotely. The calculations will be done very carefully and accurately, but they will also make absolutely no sense to anybody involved. This is possible because this corporation is always shifting people, teams and projects hierarchically around the company each year, such that it's impossible to reconcile why one area is growing so fast while another's budget is sinking without having

---

[43] Or, occasionally, Jim.

a PhD in our org structure. Therefore, none of the business owners of these budgets will actually buy-off on them when done. They'll disavow them – publicly – almost immediately."

"Huh," you remark. "Will the spreadsheets at least incorporate all of the strategies we're setting out to deploy over the next 12-18 months?"

"Only on the surface. When we do the first pass of the financials, using LY as I mentioned earlier, we will incorporate those strategies ... but the numbers will definitely roll up to be more than we can afford. We will then start a process of careful cuts to that initial roll-up, but it will eventually become a tidal wave of arbitrary tasks across all cost centers and pyramids. After we do that, there's really no telling what part of the new strategies you're talking about will have survived. It will literally be impossible to pull it apart and know for sure, even for the people who own the models."

Okay, okay – I'm beating a dead horse here. But of course this process would never get approved as described. And, yet, for 50 years that is exactly what the process has produced *at great expense* to companies both big and small. As I said above, the research suggests that the average Fortune 500 company is spending the equivalent of more than $20M annually in their budget process given the time spent by people involved! Crazy!

Eventually, this golden calf will have to go away. Instead of false budgeting, spend more time improving accountability via data & reporting enhancements and investments.

Performance Management:

If I ask a crowd of people *why* they will be doing their annual reviews in the coming year, the most frequent answer I get will sound something like this: "Because it's April."

And, yet, that's how it works in most of our companies. We don't even try to fool ourselves anymore that performance reviews are accomplishing the goals that we would naturally set out for them: assessing actual performance on the job *and* providing feedback and coaching. Nobody thinks the performance review process is going to be useful. Nobody thinks it is going to change lives or – to be frank – performance!

There is a reason why this is the case – most performance reviews are given to employees by their managers, who are bad leaders.

I would venture that 70% of all leaders in corporate America are bad leaders, and no matter how you tweak your performance process each year – on-line forms, HR involvement, longer or shorter text sections, etc. – it will not change the prism through which the review is being delivered: a bad leader.

"But," you will say to me. "My employees find these reviews very helpful each year. They look forward to them." I have bad news for you. You are either one of the 30% of good leaders or you've fooled yourself into thinking so. Either way, it doesn't change the reality that for the majority of corporate employees, the performance review process is a farce. In fact, almost 50% of employees who are owed a performance review each year never even receive one, written or oral.

And performance reviews aren't cheap. You are paying these leaders to do the work of filling out forms, rating people, etc. A study was done on Fortune 500 companies suggesting performance reviews cost these companies more than $20M in opportunity cost and another $5M in direct costs through teams that administer the process, technology to support it, storage costs, etc.

I'm going to continue to argue that the majority of people believe that performance reviews are pointless, but they do them each year because it's April. And, why do we keep doing this, when we work so hard to eliminate pointless work in all other places? Legal!

Our lawyers, another lens through which this process gets bogged down, will tell us that without reviews we can't fire people. They will say that without reviews you can't do layoffs without getting sued.

Well, I say this: You're getting sued anyway. Fuck the lawyers and do something that makes sense, that's faster and that helps your team. If any of your processes fail any one of those three tests (makes sense, happens quickly and helps the team) send it back to make it better.

Headquarters:

We continue to build monoliths to our genius in cities large-and-small across America. Amazon recently announced several billion-dollar *headquarters* locations to house its talented team. Good God!

Does this feel like the future to anybody? Is every bit of technology being developed drawing people toward the need to work in the same location in order to be productive? Not in white collar organizations, I'm sure.

It used to be that you went to offices because that's where the *best* technology was distributed. Offices had fax machines and laptops and color printers and fast internet and the latest MS Office roll-outs and more! Now, companies don't invest in those things at all. They've poured so much irretrievable money into the concrete *surrounding* their employees that they're constantly cutting funds for the technology those employees need to be productive in a modern world ... and that's only if they're not cutting money for the employees themselves!

I get it – there are all these buildings sitting around waiting for somebody to use them. So, go ahead. But if you're facing the investment of constructing a *new* building from 2015 on and you choose to do so, you're wildly deluded in how best to invest your capital.

CHAPTER TWENTY-SIX:
Putting Data in the Middle

I didn't come up with this one, but if you've been paying attention, this kind of intellectual theft hasn't stopped me before.

For twenty years companies have been told that their organizations and strategies should be built around three core aspects: People, Process and Technology. The ramifications of this are still lost on most people, but the fundamental thought worked pretty well when applied correctly.

I'm going to borrow from one of Deloitte's new constructs, though, which suggests that People, Process and Technology now all should surround a new 'core' for modern companies, that being Data.

Practically, all modern companies need to built around their data. They need to design their teams, their processes and their technology to take advantage of that data to help them evolve and protect their margins. If you are not a data-centric company here in 2019, then you are facing obsolescence whether you understand it or not.

It's time to re-orient yourselves. The Big 3 have become the Big 4, and data is the new linchpin that's here to stay.

CHAPTER TWENTY-SEVEN:
Knowledge vs. Experience

Many organizations I visit are suffering from a leadership crisis. Among those problems is the fact that too many leaders have been promoted to that level because of their *knowledge* of how the company works, whether that be the politics of the organization, the systems, the mechanics of the company's processes or whatever. Over time, these people become known: "Oh, Jane really understands how our accounts payable systems work at Acme, Inc. If she left, we'd be in real trouble because so few people know it as well as Jane. We'd better promote her to VP before another company comes along and promotes her."

Terrible.

Here's a good test to apply to this situation. It has two parts:

1) Would another company (let's call them Omega, Inc.) pay significantly for the specific knowledge that this person possesses? Remember, nothing about how Acme, Inc. has organized its systems or processes is useful for Omega, Inc. The things that would be useful to Omega would be industry information, pricing insight, competitive insight, customer preferences or more. Is that what Jane knows?

2) Is this knowledge or information part of the "secret sauce" that makes your company tick competitively? Again, I would strongly argue that how you've architected your Finance systems, bill paying, ordering or more is very unlikely to be the reason your company stays in business every day. However, if there are certain relationships with customers or vendors, this could be strategically valuable to your organization with a known risk if that information was lost. I would say the same thing about customer-facing applications or code.

Answer these two questions. If you have leaders in your organization – big or small – who you cannot answer "yes" to both of the above questions, you may be paying a **legacy executive**.

A legacy executive is somebody who has probably been with your company for a long time and helped you grow to the place you are today. They were invaluable to your organization's history, but I would suggest that value has diminished today.

Does that mean you should get rid of them? Good God, no! Or, at least, that wouldn't be my first choice.

Let's explore the challenges here. I have observed many legacy executives who helped design the systems and processes that the company uses today, and because of that role (and the knowledge that came with it) they were promoted time-and-again to executive levels.

In my definition, an executive is somebody whose impact goes above and beyond the pyramid they serve. An executive should be somebody who is hiring the best talent, developing that talent, inspiring the team and developing vision for their pyramid (or the organization in total). Legacy executives often do not do any of this – they are *core* to your business and the function they serve, but they do not reach the loftier ideals I would personally hold an executive to.

Left to these roles, legacy executives will not innovate. Why would they? They designed the very 'box' they are now working in. They know it has problems and could be better, but to fix those problems and replace that legacy would in fact cause their own value to diminish. The 'box' is what makes them what they are.

Again, it sounds like I'm advocating to remove these individuals. Not at all! They know so much about your company, its politics, processes and functional inner-workings … it's just that this insight is not being put to work toward making your company *better*! At a certain point, the c-suite team needs to approach this legacy executive and promote them to a new and important role: erasing their own legacy!

That starts by giving your legacy executive the responsibility for hiring his or her replacement and ensuring their ultimate success. In doing this, they must be measured and compensated for that successful hire and training effort. That new person must be supported, nurtured and become sustainably valuable on their own two feet. In doing *that*, your legacy executive is probably going to go face-to-face with a lot of the things he or she has just gotten used to over the years – the poor relationships, the bad processes, etc.

That leads us to the second responsibility: to seek out, identify and attack those 'legacy processes' or functions that are inhibiting your company (and their successor) from moving forward. It could be very old computer systems, relationships between pyramids that need to be improved, or anything that is blocking the company's progress.

And, they *absolutely* know what these problems are! It's at the core of how they evolved into a legacy executive. They know exactly where the skeletons are buried and what 'better' would look like for your company. They simply need the role, responsibility and compensation associated with attacking those challenges to get them to take it on.

It will make your business better.

CHAPTER TWENTY-EIGHT:

The Future of Business Education

This used to be very straight-forward: If you wanted to be successful (ie – make it to the executive ranks) in a corporate setting, you needed a college education. Oh, sure, there were exceptions to this rule, but they were relatively rare and those people could fill your heads with stories of how *not* having a degree held them back at one time or another.

And, why not? Corporations expected their entry-level employees to get educations because they were relatively cheap to acquire, had a tremendous payoff for the employee and constituted a very effective means of bifurcating applicants between people who had shown a willingness to put in the work and effort of educating themselves versus those who didn't. In an era of mass applicants for every well-paying job, why not?

For the employees, too, this was a great deal. Getting a college degree was something they had time to do as 18-year-olds, it was something that had been drilled into their heads from very young ages as the 'next step' between high school and work, and (as I already said) it was relatively inexpensive while having an amazing payback.

Personally, getting both my college education and MBA certification were the single best investments of time and money

I've ever made in my life. They weren't easy or always fun, but there is zero question that they dramatically returned value on the investment I made in them. And, since my company expected these certifications of me, why not?

For kids of that age, too, you don't have any idea what you want to be when you grow up. Spending four years of (again) relatively inexpensive time getting a college degree while spanning the years until you're emotionally ready to enter the work force was fine. I would argue that 22-year-olds largely had no skills of any usefulness when we hired them out of college *except* that they'd shown the willingness to put in the time to go to school.

All good, right?

But, has this changed? Let's attack some of these items in order.

First, college is no longer inexpensive. I am sure many of you have had children since the turn of the millennia and done the "college savings calculators" that you can find online on many websites. These calculators are supposed to help you figure out, as parents, how much to save toward your children's educations via a 529 program (or some such thing).

If you're like me and tried one of these in the mid-2000's, it told you to start putting aside something like $500 to $1,000 *per month* starting at the birth of your child! Basically, it was projecting that it was going to cost $100-200k to send your kid to school for four years. What??

And, sure enough, that seems to be how it's playing out for our Millennial (and later) graduates. These kids are coming out of school in greater debt than some first-time home buyers, and while they're encountering a job market that pays better than ever, it's by no means commensurate. Their loans and other debts are preventing them from living the same American Dream as my generation found coming out in the 90's.

And, for what? Is college keeping up with the times? I would strongly argue 'No'. With the exception of the introduction of iPads into school settings and the compulsion to add Ethics classes following the corporate scandals of the early 2000's, the college experience is largely the same as it ever has been. Stale old classrooms, stale old teachers, group projects, etc.?

How *have* colleges evolved? Well, for one, their fund-raising and endowment developing processes have gone through the roof in the last 20 years. You can't be a public or private school without having an amazing fund-raising team, and that's playing itself out. But, uh, that's about it. The kids coming out of these institutions have not progressed in relation to the price they are paying for the education.

In other words – *most* of the work-readiness effort that goes on in life is still being provided by the employers! It is these kids' first bosses, peers, mentors and experiences they get on the job that are propelling them forward toward whatever future they will have, and (largely) not the quality of education.

Now, when college cost me $8-20k per year, that was kind of acceptable. If it's costing me $30-50k per year, it's ridiculous.

So, let's sum up: Schools are more expensive, employers should be indifferent (quality has not gone up) while kids are suffering. This is all bad. So, what should be done?

Well, there are two more factors at-play that we need to introduce: One, for the first time in history, our business needs, platforms and technologies are evolving faster than education can keep up with. The fundamental changes to business that productivity tools like iPads bring to the table, along with the changes in business caused by the evolving Internet of Things, makes finding people who have skills and wherewithal to thrive in that constant turmoil all the more important to businesses. By sending these kids into the 'vacuum' of school – a place with very little emphasis on the modern, changing world – they could end up falling even farther behind the latest trends than when they started.

Two, the changing demographics of the workplace as Baby Boomers retire and the volume of replacement talent available in the market decreases (simple birth count statistics) means that the patience businesses have for workforce-ready talent is diminishing.

When you combine these two things with the stuff we covered earlier in this chapter, I think we are facing a potential for decreasing needs for education in our workforce talent. Said differently: Fuck college, we were teaching you everything you really needed to know *after* we hired you anyway, let's just get that started ASAP. If the NBA can pay these 19 year-olds millions of dollars to get started, why can't we hire earlier, too?

You will see companies start to get competitive with students *before* they finish their degrees. It will start in obvious places – IT, of course, but don't forget about Operations areas as well. Any kid who's coding his own website, managing servers or running what is (in effect) the small business of the internet will be very attractive to IT teams desperate to replenish their always depleted work forces. And, this approach will *work* - these gun-jumping corporations will find that while they have more immature team members and that there are some implications to this, they are also as talented (or more talented) than the more expensive people they're recruiting off campus.

As this begins to work, other departments will follow. The only areas I can see, over time, being required to follow an education track are those where 1) the education is simply required of fulfilling the role, such as 'brain surgeon', or 2) the returns from education continue to be high enough to pay off the debt, like *some* lawyers, doctors, tax fields, some scientific fields, etc. That's it.

Or, I'm wrong. We'll see.

AFTERWORD

I take great passion in these ideas, but I know they are not all correct. For some of them, maybe I just explained my ideas poorly. Others are just flat dumb, I'll find out over time.

Regardless, they are intended to stimulate your own ideas, much as I have taken the thoughts and considerations of others and (over the course of decades) formed my own thoughts about how things can be.

I love these conversations and I love that I'm nowhere close to done learning. If you want to start a conversation, or continue one, with me, you can find me at:

> LinkedIn: www.linkedin.com/in/brianapittenger

> E-Mail: brian.pittenger@moneybuttonbook.com

> Twitter: @PittengerEvents

Thank you for enjoying this ride with me (or not, in which case thanks for the money).

And, To all, No refunds.

ACKNOWLEDGEMENTS

Thanks to my editors at Vogt and the support staff that they've provided over the last couple years.

Thank you to all the people who've inspired me over the years. You were all called out in The Money Button, no need to repeat everything here. You're all still appreciated.

Thank you to my parents, who somehow made this kid who thinks way too much about everything.

Finally, to my wife, Pam, and my kids, Parker & Payton, who continue to be patient with me through all of this fun. *Love you all*.

Brian, Jan 2019

INDEX:

---

[i] Producers, A. Judd Apatow. Directors, A: Adam McKay. 2004. *Anchorman: The Legend of Ron Burgandy*. USA: Dreamworks.

[ii] Ferrazzi, Keith. *Never Eat Alone: And Other Secrets to Success, One Relationship at a Time*. Random House LLC, 2014 (Expanded & Updated Edition).

[iii] Taleb, Nassim Nicholas. *Antifragile*. Random House, 2012.